when you flush?

written by **Caren Trafford**
illustrated **by Jade Oakley**

"To poo or not to poo. There is no question..." Anon

Published by Etram Pty Ltd
www.planetkids.biz
www.wilburworm.com

First published in Australia 2003
2nd Edition 2004
3rd Edition 2006
Copyright
Text © Caren Trafford, 2003
Illustration © Caren Trafford, 2003

National Library of Australia
Cataloguing-in-publication entry:
Trafford, Caren
Where does the Poo go ...
ISBN 0-958-18780-0

Illustrator: Jade Oakley
Design: ANTART Design
www.antart.com.au
Printed in China through Bookbuilders

Posters available
Posters of the illustrations from this book are available from our website
www.planetkids.biz

Welcome...

Hello, my name is Goobie and I'm a big, fresh, knobbly, brown, gooey, large and steamy piece of smelly poo. At last I have the chance to tell you *my* story. Do you know how hard it is to find anyone who wants to interview a piece of poo? Let me tell you straight, it's not a piece of cake, being a piece of poo. Just think about it. If we're not being flushed down the toilet, we're being thrown in the bin, left to rot in the grass, or trampled on. And really, all we're trying to do is to make sure we are recycled. I bet you don't even know where the poo goes when you flush.
Well, let me tell you…

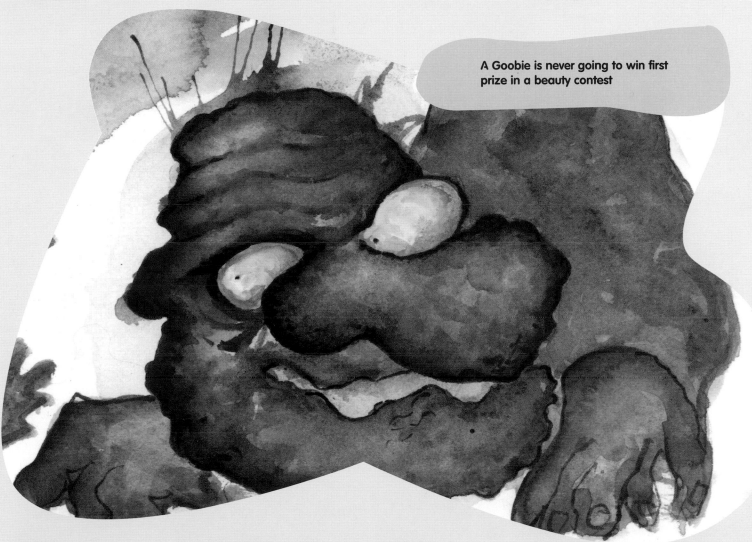

A Goobie is never going to win first prize in a beauty contest

Where there's life...there's Poo

All plants and animals are made up of tiny living cells which must eat to live. This means they have to take in nutrients, or food, to stay healthy. But, remember, what goes in, must come out and anything that has a digestive system produces poo. Poo is the undigested part of food plus a whole load of dead bacteria. I'm here to tell you what happens to the big, brown, smelly variety of poo, also known as Goobies, the distant, but solid cousins of the Bottom Burps.

Goobies love to party and are always making new friends

oobies adore
xploring and
now how to
ress for the
ccasion

How old is Poo...?

Poo has been around for a very long time. When insects and animals first occupied the planet, poo started to be dropped, here, there and everywhere.

Some early poo is considered very valuable because it has been transformed into gemstones called *Coprolites*.

Odd what humans think is valuable, isn't it?

Clues in Poo

Coprolites, or fossilised dinosaur poo can tell us about the diet and feeding patterns of prehistoric animals.

Coprolites that contain chewed leaves and pollen are from dinosaurs that ate plants. The really big dinosaurs would have eaten loads of grass to stop getting hungry. I'm glad I wasn't there then, they would have been making bottom-burps all day.

The dinosaurs that ate meat had different dino-dung. Theirs contained bone fragments and sinews. Just think, coprolites show us what, or rather, WHO, was on the menu more than 65 million years ago.

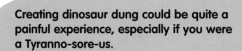

Creating dinosaur dung could be quite a painful experience, especially if you were a Tyranno-sore-us.

Poo or True?

In 1998, a 65 million year old lump of dinosaur dung was found in Canada. It was a 44 cm long, whitish-green rock from a meat-eating dinosaur, *Tyrannosaurus rex*. That's a pretty big piece of poo, even for a dinosaur. Did you know that "Saurus," means lizard?

Visiting friends could be a very slippery process

More salad anyone?

Using modern science, we can get a good idea of what ancient animals liked to eat. Poo which is less than 100,000 years old, often contains traces of DNA, (cell genetic information), that give a very accurate picture of a creature's diet. In England, a 19,000 year-old, giant ground sloth turd, was found to contain seven kinds of plant DNA, including capers, lilies, mint and grapes. Now you know what kind of salad a giant sloth loves. I wonder what type of dressing he preferred.

Free food, fertiliser and fuel

The poo that early animals dropped and plopped was recycled in Nature. Some people think that poo is just rubbish, but Nature knows that it contains lots of nutrients which feed the soil.

As the poo decomposed and broke down, it became fertiliser. The fertiliser fed the plants and made them grow; the vegetarian animals ate the plants; the predators ate the vegetarians and everyone pooed. Then, the cycle started all over again. The nutrients and poo were endlessly recycled within the soil. It was perfect. Nature was in balance.

When humans first appeared, this cycle was interrupted. Early societies began to live in groups and use fire. Humans needed fuel for their fires, so they collected and dried animal dung because it burned well.

Goobies were really busy in those early days. We helped plants to grow, practised our soft landings and were dried into fuel to create warmth and light for humans. What a full life!

What is Coprolite?

also known as fossil faeces, dinosaur dung, petrified pooh.

Coprolite means "dung stone" - "kopros" means dung and "lithikos" means stone (in Greek).

It does not smell because it has been turned to stone, or fossilised. It is rock-hard.

Coprolites record the diet and habitat of prehistoric animals.

Is it a Coprolite or just a Rock?

If the specimen contains fossilised bits of crushed and partly-digested organic material, it is not a rock, but a fossil.

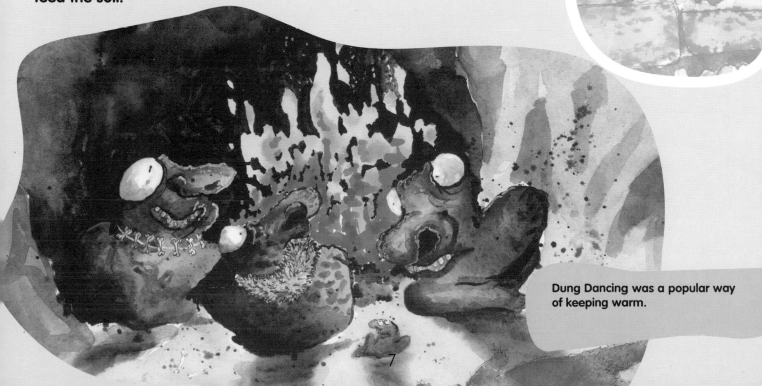

Dung Dancing was a popular way of keeping warm.

Where to do a Number 2?

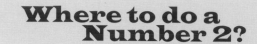

About 10,000 years ago, when people started to live in family groups or tribes, they began to go to the toilet privately - somewhere where the poo-pursuing insects would not disturb them. As time progressed, the number of people pooing increased and so did the number of Goobies. People soon realised that something needed to be done with all those Goobie piles. After all, who wanted to walk through mountains of poo when going out to hunt, or to collect berries?

Ancient Loos for Ancient Poos...

The first toilets, were little more than holes in the ground. When they were full, humans simply dug another hole and started over again.

Research shows that pulling faces started back in ancient times

Candles or 'Goobie Gaslights' were important - you never knew who was going to drop in next

Poo or True?

Did you know that humans are thought to be the only creatures that can wipe their bottoms with toilet paper? It is believed that the first way people wiped their bottoms was with leaves and sticks. Some cultures today, use their left hand and a water hose to clean their backsides. Perhaps this is why we shake hands with our right hand?

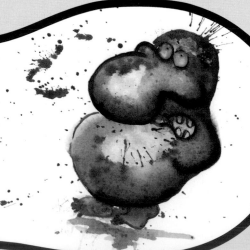

First Movements in Plumbing

4000-3000 B.C
India: Copper water pipes found in palace ruins in the Indus River Valley.

2500 B.C
Egypt: Intricate bathrooms were built inside pyramids for the dead to use on their journey to the after-life. The Egyptians also developed elaborate irrigation and sewage systems using copper pipe.

2400-2150 B.C
Ancient Babylon: A network of canals and large brick drainage sewers with access holes like today's manholes were constructed.

1500 B.C
Crete: Fresh water systems, sewage systems and flushing toilets were common.

500 B.C - 455 A.D
The Roman Empire: The Romans built aquaducts and pools with hot and cold water.

They also built large public toilets with marble seats over running water channels. This continual flow of water allowed the Goobies to flush away. Sponges attached to long sticks allowed the customers to wipe their bottoms.

The expression, "to get hold of the wrong end of the stick," is thought to have originated at this time.

What to do with all that Poo?

For thousands of years, people had very different attitudes towards Goobies.

In some countries, Goobies were valued as a fantastic source of fertiliser. We were collected and spread over crops to help them grow.

In other parts of the world, attitudes developed differently. Goobies were seen as a stinking nuisance, to be tossed away as quickly as possible. Rather than being appreciated as a valuable fertiliser, people believed Goobies were a dirty, smelly problem.

Plop.. Stop..

So the big question is, are Goobies good or bad? Well, they're both!

Goobies, (poo, poop, number 2s...), are the body's waste products. Everything you eat or drink is broken down inside your body, so that it can be used for energy and nourishment. The left-overs and waste are then broken down by millions of bacteria that live inside you. As they do this, they also make gases and chemicals. That's why Goobies smell!

What comes out of your butt is a cocktail mixture of gases, chemicals, leftovers and millions of tiny bacteria. These are great for the soil, but some of the bugs can make you sick if you eat them. So, when you do a poo in the loo, (or anywhere else for that matter), always wash your hands.

To poo or not to poo - Romans thought a lot about this question

Goobies discover travel

In ancient Greece and Italy, great cities such as Athens and Rome, were built. As the population grew so did the number of Goobies.

Goobies, as you know, don't have legs. We don't even roll. We just love to lounge around, being smelly. But, the construction of Goobie slides in the ancient world, allowed us to slip and slither away, rather than just lie about like pooey couch potatoes....weeeee

Archaeologists have discovered huge networks of pipes and tunnels under the ancient cities. These were built to carry fresh water into the houses and waste and Goobies out of them.

It is reported that one of the most famous water-slides in Goobie history was under the home of the ruler of Rome: Caesar's Palace. Many a young Goobie and Bottie-Burp enjoyed these first slippery dips; shooting the curves and racing each other through the sewers.

Of course, they went in one direction only – down. Gravity was the natural power that carried the waste through the early sewers. As we all know, water flows down to the lowest point, but unfortunately the lowest point is normally a river, a lake, or the ocean.

A crucial part of a Goobie's education is learning to swim

Poo or True?

The word, "Plumber" comes from Roman times and derives from the Latin words, *artifex plumbarius* meaning, 'worker in lead'. Many Roman water pipes were made from lead.

The *Baths of Diocletian* were the largest in Rome. 3,000 bathers could bathe there at the same time. They covered 13 hectares (32 acres), had changing rooms, gymnasiums, libraries, meeting rooms, theatres, concert halls, sculpture gardens and vast basins for hot, lukewarm and cold plunges.

In ancient Rome, all the Goobies in the sewers flowed down into the great Tiber River which is quite famous in Roman legends. It is said that people would swim in it as a test of courage.

However, all that sewage in the river meant one thing, pollution. The Tiber was no longer fit to drink. (Remember Goobies also contain bad bugs that make people sick if the bugs are swallowed).

The Romans were great builders. To fix the pollution problem that they had created, they built giant water roads which brought fresh water from the rivers and lakes in the mountains down to the city of Rome. These were called aquaducts, (bridges carrying water) and one was even a double-decker.

Unfortunately the Romans never understood the value of human poo. Once in the Tiber, the poo flowed down-river and into the sea. What a waste. Perhaps it was the Roman's fault that even today, 2,000 years later, very little human poo is used in farming.

Spending time in the water is a favourite hobby among Goobies

The end of water sliding competitions

After almost 1,000 years, the Roman Empire crumbled and life in the fast lane for the Goobies came to an abrupt halt. What a pity - we had been having so much fun, sliding through all the pipes and sewers built by the first Roman plumbers.

In 538 A.D invading Goths cut off Rome's water by demolishing the aquaducts. The 900 Baths in Rome could no longer be used as there was no water. The Goths were basic people and thought very little about bathing and flush toilets. With the destruction of Rome, the civilization and plumbing that had been invented was forgotten. According to my ancestor, *Romanus Goobilanium*, it was back to the roadside '*plop and flop*' once more.

Once the Goths took over and the Roman Baths were destroyed, everyone was in the poo

Back to basics

For the next 1,000 years, the Western world sank into what has been called, *The Dark Ages*. During this time, many different wild tribes swept through Europe, destroying or stealing anything of value. Most of the knowledge of the ancient civilisations was lost. There was no internet, no TV, very few books and schooling was limited to the very rich and the church community.

What happened? For hundreds of years, the sewage systems, clean baths and toilets that had been widely used in Rome during the 4th and the 5th centuries, were forgotten. Goobies were left to play by the road-sides and pile up outside people's houses.

Poo or True?
They were called 'The Dark Ages,' because:

1. there was no electricity
2. it was cloudy
3. nobody washed and everyone was very dirty

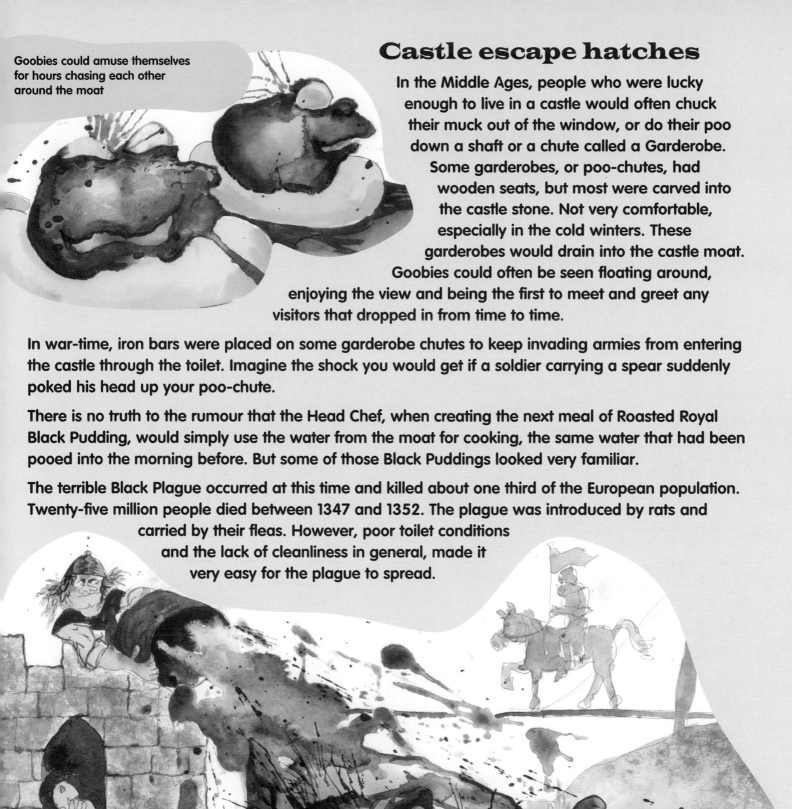

Goobies could amuse themselves for hours chasing each other around the moat

Castle escape hatches

In the Middle Ages, people who were lucky enough to live in a castle would often chuck their muck out of the window, or do their poo down a shaft or a chute called a Garderobe. Some garderobes, or poo-chutes, had wooden seats, but most were carved into the castle stone. Not very comfortable, especially in the cold winters. These garderobes would drain into the castle moat. Goobies could often be seen floating around, enjoying the view and being the first to meet and greet any visitors that dropped in from time to time.

In war-time, iron bars were placed on some garderobe chutes to keep invading armies from entering the castle through the toilet. Imagine the shock you would get if a soldier carrying a spear suddenly poked his head up your poo-chute.

There is no truth to the rumour that the Head Chef, when creating the next meal of Roasted Royal Black Pudding, would simply use the water from the moat for cooking, the same water that had been pooed into the morning before. But some of those Black Puddings looked very familiar.

The terrible Black Plague occurred at this time and killed about one third of the European population. Twenty-five million people died between 1347 and 1352. The plague was introduced by rats and carried by their fleas. However, poor toilet conditions and the lack of cleanliness in general, made it very easy for the plague to spread.

One of the most popular weapons in the Middle Ages was known as the "Goobie-Grabber"

13

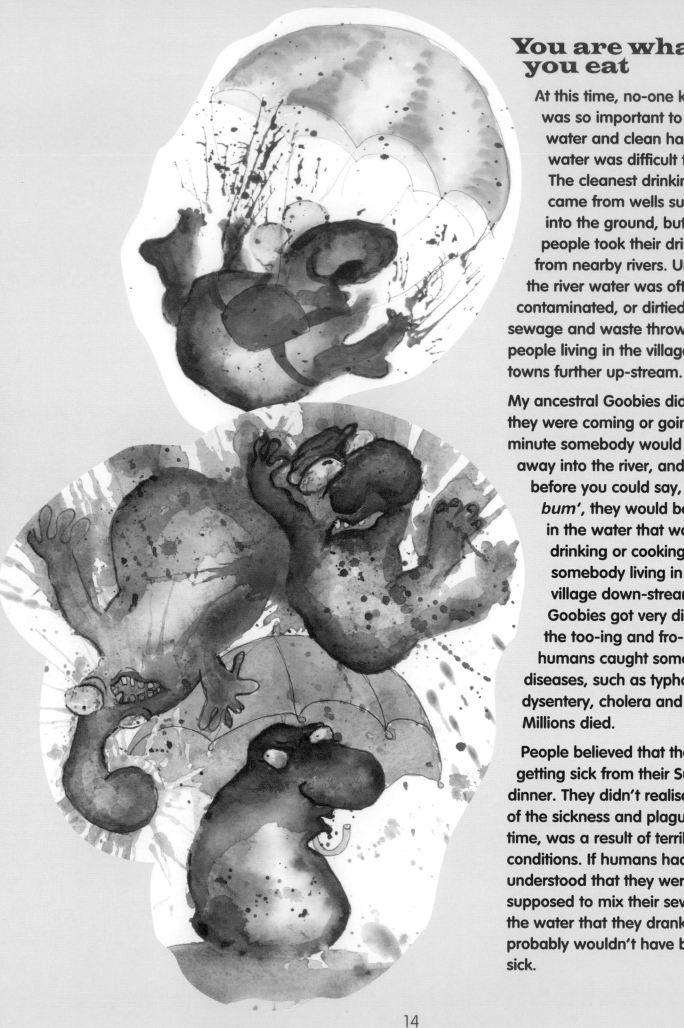

You are what you eat

At this time, no-one knew why it was so important to have clean water and clean hands. Fresh water was difficult to collect. The cleanest drinking water came from wells sunk deep into the ground, but many people took their drinking water from nearby rivers. Unfortunately, the river water was often contaminated, or dirtied, from the sewage and waste thrown there by people living in the villages and towns further up-stream.

My ancestral Goobies didn't know if they were coming or going. One minute somebody would throw them away into the river, and then, before you could say, *'itchy-bum'*, they would be collected in the water that was used for drinking or cooking, by somebody living in the town or village down-stream. Those Goobies got very dizzy from all the too-ing and fro-ing, and the humans caught some terrible diseases, such as typhoid, dysentery, cholera and hepatitis. Millions died.

People believed that they were getting sick from their Sunday dinner. They didn't realise that much of the sickness and plague at this time, was a result of terrible hygiene conditions. If humans had understood that they weren't supposed to mix their sewage with the water that they drank, they probably wouldn't have become so sick.

Which diseases can people catch if they come into contact with Untreated Poo?

Cholera

Spread by contaminated water or food.

It causes a large amount of watery diarrhoea which can lead to severe dehydration (lack of water in the body) or death.

Typhoid

An infection caused by bacteria which are transmitted from poo to the stomach.

People become infected after eating or drinking foods that have been handled by a person who is infected, or by drinking water that has been contaminated by sewage containing the bacteria.

There are about 17 million cases worldwide, per year.

Hepatitis A

This virus causes an infection of the liver. It is passed in a person's poo and can then be carried on an infected person's hands. It is spread by eating food or drink that has been handled by the infected person.

It can also be spread by drinking water contaminated with improperly treated sewage.

Diarrhoea

Diarrhoea is caused by a host of bacteria and organisms most of which are spread by contaminated (dirty) water.

Animal poo also contains bacteria that can cause diarrhoea.

World-wide around 1.1 billion people, (1 in 6) lack access to proper water sources and 2.4 billion have no basic sanitation or hygiene.

In 1998, diarrhoea was estimated to have killed 2.2 million people, most of whom were under 5 years of age (World Health Organisation, 2000). Each year there are approximately 4 billion cases of diarrhoea worldwide.

Dysentery

Dysentery is diarrhoea containing blood. The most likely way to get it is by person-to-person contact and consuming contaminated water and food.

Ascariasis

An infection of the small intestine caused by a large roundworm. The worm's eggs are found in soil contaminated by human poo, or in uncooked food infected by soil containing the worm's eggs.

The female adult worm can grow to over 30cm in length. They lay eggs that are then passed into the poo: one is infected by swallowing the eggs.

Goobies come clean

I have a little confession to make about Goobies. Even though we are really great guys - caring, sensitive, playful, happy to do the washing-up; not everything about a Goobie is good. Over the ages we have been responsible for quite a lot of sickness, disease and even death. It is very important for Goobies to be properly treated and for you to always WASH YOUR HANDS after doing a poo.

Goobies, like humans, need to be looked after and treated with respect.

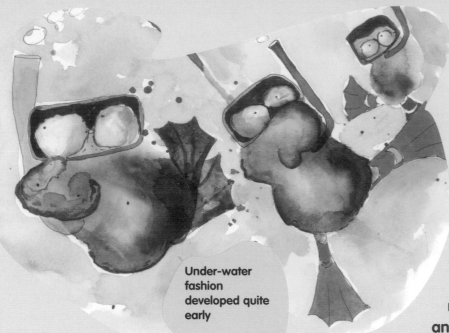

Western Poo History: stay or take-away

The flush toilet that we use today has only become popular in the last 100 years. Before that, it was normal to dispose of poo on dry land by burying it.

In the medieval cities of England and Europe poo was considered to be a nuisance and of no value, certainly not something that could be recycled. The most common way of getting rid of poo and waste was to drop it into the "pit", also known as the "communal toilet", or "privy". This was just a hole in the ground, sometimes with a wooden or stone seat at the top. The stories of the wonderful smelly times and adventures that Goobies had in those dark, deep holes have been written up in the infamous encyclo-poo-dia, *Poo-i-us*, section IV, a), "The Dark Ages…".

When the poo pit was full, it was either dug out - *(O.K. hands up for that job),* cleaned and the poo was hauled off by the 'gong farmer', or if there was room, it was covered up and a new pit was dug nearby. Then the whole process was repeated.

There were a number of problems with this way of dealing with poos and Number 2s. Can you guess what they were?

Many pits were too small for their contents and frequently overflowed. Even worse, people sometimes fell through the rotten boards that covered the pit and drowned. What a frightening experience that was for us Goobies!

Under-water fashion developed quite early

The expression,' to dive in head first,' was used a lot at this time

Poo or True?

One of the highest courts in England is called the Privy Council. It is the council that advises the Queen or King on matters of state. What else do you think they discuss there?

In the U.S, Governors run for election at the Goobie- natorial. The word comes from the Latin *gubernare* to steer, govern, and is usually spelt, "Gubernatorial."

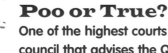

Eastern Poo History...early recycling

While history tells of how Goobies were misunderstood in the majority of Europe, thankfully, in other parts of the world we were considered useful.

In many places in the East, we were shovelled together and used as fertiliser. In China, poo was called 'night soil' and the Chinese Goobies were spread out over the surrounding farmland to fertilise the crops and help them to grow. The crops were sold in near-by cities, while the waste from those cities was returned to the farms. This type of system worked brilliantly because two problems were solved at once; finding a fertiliser, and getting rid of waste. I have heard that 'night soil' was so valuable that farmers competed with one another by building eye-catching toilets, or out-houses, along roads to tempt passers-by to use them.

And that's not all! We also had great fun in Persia (now called Iran). About 700 years ago, a great sewage system was built near a city called Isfehan. All the sewage was collected in a giant underground cistern or cellar. The roof of the cellar was curved and at the top of the curve there was a small hole.

I don't know if you know, but Goobies love to get together. When they do, a family of bacteria, called anaerobes (bacteria that don't need oxygen), break down the Goobies and produce a fantastic gas called methane and some really smelly other gases. Methane is like the gas you cook with. And this is what the ancient Persians did. They lit the gas as it came out of the little hole at the top of the underground tank and used the flame to heat water for the city. WOW!

Evolution of Modern Sewerage Systems in the Western World

538: Disappearance of piped water in Rome after the Goths invaded the city.

1200: Piped water systems started to be built in some British cities. These carried clean water to public fountains.

1388: In England, an act of Parliament "forbade the throwing of filth and garbage into ditches, rivers, and water".

1500s: Laws passed forbidding anyone to bury poo and sewage within the City of London.

1596: First Flushing Toilet (Water Closet). Built by Sir John Harrington, godson to Queen Elizabeth I of England. It was called a "necessary" but it was laughed at by his friends. He never built another one.

1728: First sewer built under the streets of New York.

1739: First separate toilets for men and women in Paris.

1819: Albert Giblin patented the *Silent Valveless Water Waste Preventer* in Britain. This system allowed a toilet to flush effectively.

1824: First Public Toilet in Paris.

1850s: First city sewers constructed in Sydney, Australia. They drained straight out into the harbour in front of the current site of the Opera House.

1854: Dr. John Snow (England) proved the connection between cholera and bad sanitation.

1857: Toilet-paper is thought to have been invented by an American, Joseph Coyetty.

1858: Known as the 'Year of the Great Stink' in the U.K. Led to changes in the law regarding sewage disposal.

1859: Toilet of Queen Victoria of England is decorated with gold.

1861: Thomas Crapper obtained patent rights from Albert Gilpin for his flush toilet invention and began commercial production of toilets.

1880: 'British Perforated Paper Company' manufactured toilet paper which came in boxes of small pre-cut squares.

Goobies take flying lessons

As towns increased in size towards the end of the Middle Ages and multi-storey houses were built, the hygiene problem grew worse. When people started to live upstairs, they were far enough from the ground to empty their waste and their Goobie pots out of the window into the streets below. This was the time that Goobies first started to take flying lessons and pretty soon, we were able to land quite accurately on the passers-by below. Weee…- splat!

You never knew WHO you were going to land on next. No wonder everyone wore BIG hats. When it rained the Goobies raced into the open sewers that ran down the middle of the streets. These would drain into the nearest stream or river. Although medieval Europeans did not understand how disease could be carried in polluted water, they were aware that drinking the water would often result in illness. Many people refused to drink water, preferring to drink ale or wine. *I know a few people like that nowadays.* People rarely bathed and the rich used perfumes to cover up their rather unpleasant smells.

Poo or True?
'Gardyloo' (from the French *regardez l'eau* 'watch out for the water.') was the cry from medieval servants as they emptied the chamber-pots out of upstairs windows into the street. It is believed that this may be the origin of the English word "loo" for a toilet.

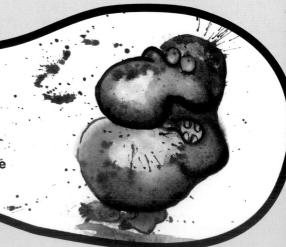

So you can see that for many hundreds of years in Western society, Goobies had a free hand. It was wonderful. We learnt to fly as we were chucked out of windows; took surfing lessons on the open sewers and provided food for fish in rivers and streams.

Our free and easy life continued until the mid 19th century, when in some places, pipes or sewers were built, to separate human's waste from their drinking water.

In Europe, in the 19th century, an outbreak of the disease cholera finally led to the discovery of a connection between cholera and dirty drinking water.

The result was the introduction of closed sewers. This made sure that my fellow Goobies were kept out of the drinking water, but it would be at least another 100 years before humans were ready to put Goobies to any really good use.

Poo or True?

What type of wipe do you like?

Often, where you lived determined how you would clean your bottom.
In coastal regions, mussels were popular
In Hawaii, they used coconut shells
In the Middle East, the left hand is preferred
In Colonial America, corn cobs were favoured
But, in the West, when daily newspapers became fashionable, paper became the first choice.

What happens to all that Poo?

It depends where you are. Today, there are some pretty complex ways of getting rid of poo, so there are many choices for Goobies.

We start our lives by either being dropped down a hole, usually if you live in the countryside; washed into a septic tank - if your home is not on the sewerage system, - or being flushed down the toilet.

Once we are flushed, we float down the pipes and sometimes, we meet other objects of interest on the way - onion rings, tea leaves, bath-water bubbles, you'd be surprised what humans wash down the sink, laundry, bath and shower. Some of the strangest things are flushed down the toilet. In the pipes, under the streets, we meet up with Goobies and waste from other houses and together, we start our journey, towards the nearest sewerage treatment plant.

In case you are feeling confused, sewage is the term used to describe the mixture of water and human waste. Sewerage system is the term used for the network of pipes that carries sewage to a sewerage treatment plant.

Goobies like to dress up when leaving the house

The sewerage system (which carries waste-water) is made up of networks of different sized pipes. The smaller ones are called service branch lines (*imagine taking a local train*). Then there are the reticulation mains (*bigger pipes like taking a regional train service*); maintenance holes (*manholes - imagine these as stations where you can get a quick repair if you need one*); pump stations (*designed to take us up hills*) and trunk sewers (*these are the inter-city monster pipes*) that take us to the sewerage plant. Some of the pipes are so big that humans can walk through them. I guess that's quite important, especially if they spring a leak or need to be inspected.

Most sewage pipes are built on a slight slope downwards to use gravity. It's free! So how do we get up all those hills? By pump. There are pumping stations at the bottom of hills which give us a bit of a boost, a little like getting on an escalator in a shopping centre. It's much easier than having to walk, especially if you are a Goobie and don't have any feet.

Did you know that sewage is mostly water and contains very little solids - usually less than 0.1%? It is these solids - mostly other Goobies - that need to be removed and treated so they can be recycled. This is what happens at the Sewerage Treatment Plant.

Goobies love sliding through the ups and downs of life

You never know whose butt you will bump at the sewerage treatment plant

Why do we treat sewage waste?

At the beginning of the 20th century, engineers needed to decide whether to separate the sewage from water or, to let it dilute in water and flow straight into lakes, rivers and oceans.

By 1910, the most common way to get rid of sewage was to dump it into water.

Towns drawing their drinking water downstream from sewage discharges began to have typhoid outbreaks.

When cities started to filter and disinfect the drinking water, the typhoid decreased.

Under pressure of industrialisation, money was invested to provide sewage systems for both homes and factories.

As a result, the nutrients in poo became mixed with industrial wastes. These were often poisonous or toxic.

In the 1950s, waters receiving sewage piped wastes had become badly polluted.

Environmental concern led to public demands to clean or treat waste before it was dumped.

This was done: but with 100s of sewerage treatment plants producing toxic sludge in huge quantities, the question was what to do with all the sewage?

Research provided the answers.

What do Goobies do in their spare time?

Having built sewerage treatment plants all around the world, humans found themselves needing to get rid of tonnes and tonnes of biosolids, (processed de-watered poo). The problem was what to do with all of it? It just kept coming.

Before people got smart, some coastal cities dumped their sewage sludge into the oceans. This created large areas that did not support aquatic life and where you could not swim. Other communities dumped their sludge into landfills, where it polluted the groundwater and made greenhouse gases. Still others incinerated or burnt their sludge and created serious air poo-llution problems.

My fellow Goobies, at this time, were very miserable. They knew how useful they could

be, but no-one was listening. "Use us, we want to help!" they would say. But no! Goobies were seen as worthless. We had no friends and no influence. Nobody wanted us.

Luckily this unhappy state of affairs did not last. Gradually humans realised that their environment was being damaged by allowing biosolids, (my de-watered friends and relatives), to flow into the oceans, or by dumping them in landfill. As a result of some environmental friendly encouragement and legislation, the true value of poo was researched and realised.

Today, Goobies have a much happier story to tell. Now, after visiting the sewerage treatment plant and being turned into not-so-smelly, stable, dryish lumps of sludge cake, there are all sorts of places that we can end up.....

What is sewage?

Sewage is the wastewater released by residences, businesses and industries in a community. It is more than 99% water, with less than 1% percent wastewater.

Are all sewerage treatment plants the same?

No, there are many different types of sewerage treatment plants. The type of plant will depend on where it is located, what sewage it needs to treat, how many people live in the region etc.

Why do we need to treat sewage?

Pathogens or disease-causing organisms are present in sewage. These need to be got rid of before the sewage can be released back into the environment. The goal is to reduce or remove organic matter, solids, nutrients, disease-causing organisms and other pollutants from the wastewater.

Now there are many different processes available to turn your sewage into a safe and useful mixture while at the same time reclaim millions of litres of water.

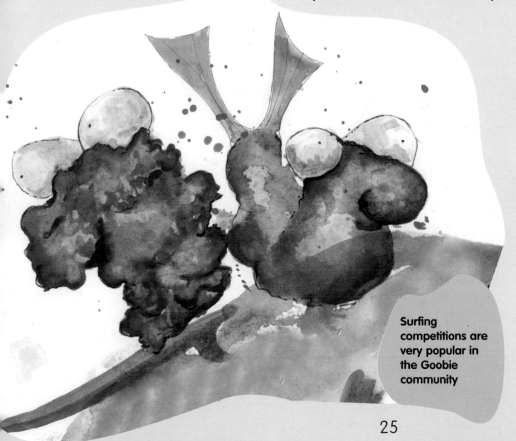

Surfing competitions are very popular in the Goobie community

What Happens at a Sewerage Treatment Plant?

1: Everything entering the sewerage plant is screened so that the plant machinery is not damaged. Sticks, rags, sand, toys, dead animals & plastic bags are removed by passing everything through giant screens (sieves).The rubbish collected is usually disposed of in a landfill.

2: The mixture (sludge) is then aerated. This is when good bacteria (tiny organisms) are used to break down and eat the sludge. The air-loving bugs feed on the sludge and purify the wastewater. Aeration can take from 4 hours to several days, during which time the sludge breaks down. It is then carried to the clarifier.

3: In the clarifier, the solid particles in the mixture are attracted together and settle to the bottom, separating from the wastewater. The water can then be diverted. This water will still have lots of nutrients in it. The next stage is to make sure that the nutrients are removed before the water is released back into the environment. Various methods may be used to "clean" the water including sand filters, reed beds, grass plots and disinfection.

4: The solids can now either go straight to the de-watering process, (in this case the belt-press (6)), or flow onto the Digester. Digesters are used to reduce the volume of sludge. They are giant enclosed tanks, mostly made of concrete where anaerobic bugs eat the sludge producing methane and other gases. The methane is used as energy for the plant and the other gases are trapped so as to not cause bad smells.

5: The water leaving the Digester is cleaned to remove collected nutrients before it is released back into the environment. One way to clean the water is by using "engineered" reed beds. Next time you see a dam or a river, look for the reed beds on the water's edge. This is Nature's way of filtering the water.

6: The solids have some chemicals added to them to help remove further water (dewater). Then the solids are put through a belt press which squeezes out most of the water. This water is returned to the sewerage treatment plant to be processed again.
The end product - sludge cake - is then piled up, ready for its next adventure… to be recycled.

27

Recycling - your end is a new beginning

My favourite hobby is to make a list and pick where to go to be recycled. Should it be…

worm farms,
road fill,
energy,
compost,
fertiliser, electricity, forests or agriculture,
bricks or gas?

Now that scientists and engineers have discovered how to remove many of the chemicals that Goobies used to contain, the Goobies, when they leave the sewerage treatment plant have a huge choice of where they can go to be recycled safely.

The biosolid or Goobie mixture is full of nutrients, such as nitrogen and phosphorus, which plants love. One choice for us, is to be spread safely back onto the land. We are also fantastic for plants as the Goobie nutrients help them grow at astonishing rates.

My best Goobie friend, *Erky*, recently went to a huge pumpkin and tomato farm where he had a superb time. First he rode in a huge truck, and then he was spread out, all over the field. He had a lovely view.

A couple of weeks later, the pumpkin that he had helped to grow, won first prize at a very important garden show,

This morning I got a postcard from my cousin *Yuckie*, who is spending his summer at a worm farm. Worms love to eat Goobies and waste and they turn us into a fantastically yummy food or soil conditioner for plants, called vermicast. It makes everything grow poo-fectly.

It really is quite difficult these days to decide where to go to be recycled.

Some of my friends get turned into road fill; others who are a little more square take a trip to the brick factory and are made into bricks; I even know some bright sparks who end up being converted into electricity.

Then, there are my really COOL friends who live at the incinerator. They get heated up and turned into the energy which powers the whole plant. Imagine, a little Goobie being converted into energy.... WOW. What poo-wer!

Goobies are like butterflies - they love the outdoors and don't like being chased by nets

29

A last word....

Next time you flush, remember how through the ages, where there's been life, there have been Goobies.

Now, with billions of people and animals on one little planet, it is more important than ever to protect the environment and keep it clean.

"The only thing that should go down the loo is a Number 1 or a Number 2!"

After reading my story, you would have to agree that Goobies have been far more active than you ever thought possible.

However, it is thanks to recycling, that Goobies are now having some of their best adventures.

There's a lot to do if you're born a poo!

So remember next time you flush, YOUR poo might end up; keeping you warm, growing your food, creating a road for you to travel on, or even building your next house.

I'm sure to see you around.......again.....soon....

Some Poo Facts that may surprise you

- One flush of your toilet uses as much water as the average person in the developing world uses for a whole day's washing, cleaning, cooking and drinking.

- An average person visits the toilet 2500 times a year. About 6-8 times a day.

- You spend about 3 years of your life on the toilet.

- In developed countries, 40% of the water we use each day is flushed down the toilet, and another 35% is used in showers and baths.

- In a year, the average person can pass a tonne of poo.

- 1 in 6 people in the world does not have access to clean drinking water and 1 in 3 does not have access to adequate sanitary conditions.

Poo or True?

In Paris, dog poo is so common that more than 600 people a year are reported to be hospitalised after slipping on dog poo on the footpath.

LEGEND

A3 Pooed by dinosaur and turned into precious fossil called Coprolite
- to C2

A6 Worms dig short-cut to pit
- to C7

A8 Thrown on fire and discover fire-dancing
- to B10

A13 Goobie uses favourite orange flippers and unblocks pipe
- to B12

B14 Bathroom built at far end of pyramid
- to A12

B11 Roman gets wrong end of stick
- to A10

B5 Water slide springs leak
- to A4

B3 Shorter showers mean less waste
- to D5

C3 Poo pit overflow - mind the puddles
- to A5

C6 Invent non drip tap
- to D7

C9 Roman aquaduct destroyed by Goths
- to A11

C12 Design water system to pipe shower water to garden
- to D13

D14 New snorkel design for active Goobies
- to F12

D11 Bathroom tap drips
- to B8

Introducing PIPES & LEAKS: The Great Game for 2 or more players

"Hi there.... it's me....GOOBIE. My friends and I are stuck at **A1** on this Board. Can you help us? We want to get to the Recycling GOOBIE CUP. All you have to do is throw one dice and move the correc number of squares. If you land on a PIPE... Yippee... you can climb up it but if you land on a LEAK...

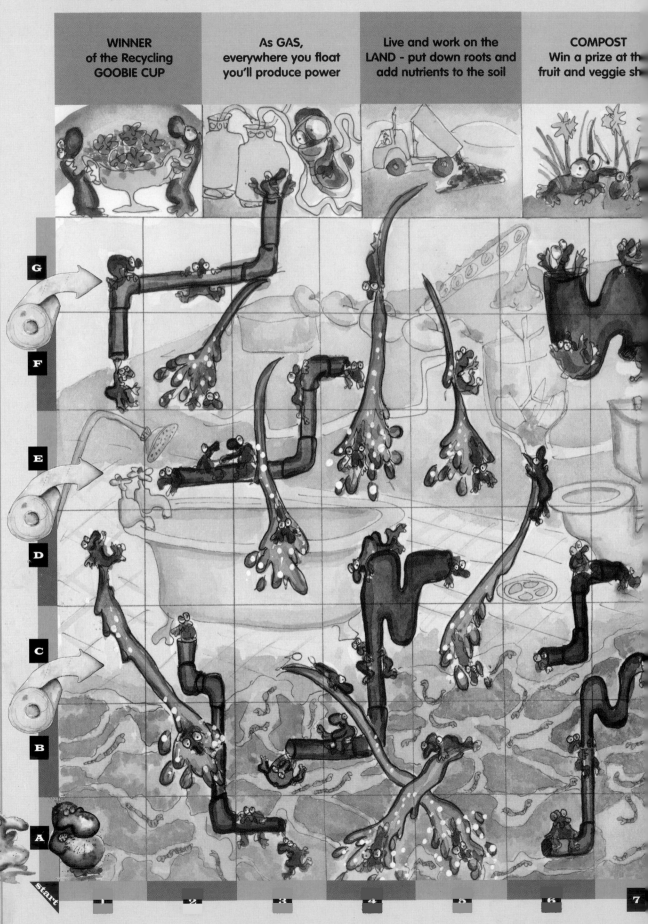

WINNER of the Recycling GOOBIE CUP

As GAS, everywhere you float you'll produce power

Live and work on the LAND - put down roots and add nutrients to the soil

COMPOST Win a prize at th fruit and veggie sh

Start